The Boy From Nine Miles

The Boy From Nine Miles

THE EARLY LIFE OF BOB MARLEY

CEDELLA MARLEY

GERALD HAUSMAN

art by MARIAH FOX

HR
for the evolving human spirit

HAMPTON ROADS
PUBLISHING COMPANY, INC.

Cover design by Grace Pedalino
Cover art by Mariah Fox
Permission for all lyrics is granted by Bob Marley Music
Photographic credit for Marley family photo: Bob Marley Music
Photographic credit for Cedella Marley photo: Bob Marley Music
Photographic credit for Gerald Hausman photo: Bobbe Besold
Photographic credit for Mariah Fox photo: NCL

Hampton Roads Publishing Company, Inc.
1125 Stoney Ridge Road
Charlottesville, VA 22902

434-296-2772
fax: 434-296-5096
e-mail: hrpc@hrpub.com
www.hrpub.com

If you are unable to order this book from your local
bookseller, you may order directly from the publisher.
Call 1-800-766-8009, toll-free.

Library of Congress Catalog Card Number: 2001098000
ISBN 1-57174-282-4
10 9 8 7 6 5 4 3 2 1
Printed on acid-free paper in China

LIVICATION:

Thanks to my grandma, my mom, all my sisters and brothers, and nieces and nephews, Danny, and my true inspiration . . . Soul-Rebel and Skip.

Cedella Marley

To Cedella and all of our friends and family in Jamaica.

Gerald Hausman
Mariah Fox

NINE MILES

Nesta Robert Marley was born in the village of Nine Miles in the Parish of St. Ann, Jamaica. His mother Ciddy was so proud that February morning and so were his grandfather Omeriah and his grandmother Alberta, in whose house Nesta opened his eyes to the world.

On the windowsill in the warm winter sun, three little birds came to sing their sweet songs. "It is a sign," said Ciddy. Omeriah, who was known all around as a seer, nodded and said, "I think that a new day is dawning." And the song of the three little birds and the news of the birth traveled throughout the hilltop town of Nine Miles.

When Nesta was five years old, he worked every day in the planting fields with his grandfather. They would set out with pail and hoe in the early morning sun, and always as they walked up the rumpled hills to the farm, Nesta asked, "Where is my daddy today?" And Omeriah replied, "Oh, your father is wearing his tall boots somewhere."

To Nesta this meant that Captain Norval Marley was riding his great white horse and doing great work in the service of his country. In truth, Nesta had only seen his father once, and never so close that he could rest his eyes upon him easily or call him by his name. Never once had he said Daddy to the Captain's face. Moreover, he could not imagine doing so.

Young Nesta soon forgot about his absent father. Instead he thought about the man he knew and loved, his grandfather, Omeriah. Together, the two worked under the shade of Omeriah's large straw hat. They weeded and widened the rows of corn, yam, and potato. And all the while, Omeriah spoke of things the boy liked to hear, and Nimble the donkey snorted in the shade and twitched his ears.

Amidst the song of grasshopper and cricket, Nesta listened while his grandfather spoke deep and clear, and his hoe clinked against the stones. In the risen sun he told Nesta of African kings and biblical patriarchs, and these legendary folk rose taller than the tallest clouds and they cast long blue shadows across the green folded ground of Nine Miles.

While Omeriah told stories, Nesta saw Goliath grow out of a thunderhead in the sky, and Nesta imagined that he was David. When that cloud crumbled away another appeared in its place. The next one was Samson charging the Philistines with a donkey's jawbone clutched in his hand. One day Omeriah was telling of the three men who jumped out of the fire—Shadrack, Meshack, and Abednego—when up the steep red road came a high-booted man on a big white horse. Nesta was thinking of the fire-jumpers, who outwitted the king, Nebuchadnezzar. For a moment, he failed to see that the horseman was his father, Captain Marley.

That night, when Ciddy tucked Nesta into his bed, she told him what his father's visit was all about. "My precious boy," she said, "you are going to get a wonderful opportunity—you are going away to school!" Nesta drew a deep breath. Then he asked, "When, Mumma?"

"Tomorrow," she said, stroking his head. She smiled as if the certainty of this thing were carved in stone. "Will I leave Nine Miles?" Nesta asked. And Ciddy replied, "Yes, child, it is all arranged by your father. You will get your schooling in Kingston. There you will learn to read and write and speak proper English." Nesta's eyes filled with tears, but he did not cry. He saw the look in his mother's eyes, and he knew there was no sense in trying to talk her out of it. The thing was done and his father had done it.

Sometime after the kerosene lantern went out in the next room, Nesta lay awake. The sleeping house dreamed—but little Nesta tossed and turned. He did not want to go to Kingston. Most of all he did not want to go with his father, the stranger who wore a uniform and who called him Robert, and whom he never called Daddy.

In the muffled stillness of his grandfather's house, Nesta closed his eyes and a vision came to him. He saw a pale rider come over the high hill on a pale horse. And that man was sorrow. Down the hill and into the village the sad horseman came, and the hooves of his white horse echoed against the houses.

When he opened his eyes, it was morning. Ciddy laid out his traveling clothes. Clean overalls, a crisp cotton shirt, and something he never wore at all—shoes. These he put on with some difficulty, they felt terrible and hot on his feet. When Alberta placed a bowl of cornmeal porridge in front of Nesta, he ate it in silence, watching the john crows float lazily past the open window. After finishing his breakfast, Nesta went outside where Omeriah gave him a stick of fresh-cut sugar cane to take with him on his trip.

Nesta thought of all the mornings with Omeriah, and a tear slid down his cheek. Quickly he wiped it away. Omeriah said, "Do not look so cast out, Nesta. Go like David into the lion's den. Fearful of nothing and with nothing to fear." Omeriah rubbed Nesta's head and, all together, the family walked up the red road to meet Captain Marley at the bus stop.

The Captain was waiting for them but he was not atop his white horse. Right away, Nesta noticed how polished were his boots. But he did not dare to look into his father's eyes, yet neither did the tall man look down into his. Presently, the heavily packed country bus bumbled round the corner and ground to a stop. A cloud of rust-colored dust came up from the road and settled on the bus and all the people in it.

Captain Marley grabbed Nesta's hand and swept him up on to the bus. Nesta found himself smothered in the noise of neighbors and strangers. Outside the bus, Omeriah, Alberta and Ciddy waved goodbye. Omeriah said, "Walk good!" Alberta reminded, "Nuh forget your manners!" Ciddy reached through the open window and touched his hand. She was crying and Nesta cried out to her. The bus lurched forward, and started to leave. Captain Marley's hand tightened. Then all that Nesta knew and loved went away like a summer's dream. Nine Miles was lost to sight. The paths and gullies that Nesta had traveled upon with Nimble wound away and were gone, and Nine Miles was no more.

KINGSTON

Nesta's eyes stayed on the road, as if it were his only friend. He watched the surface change from dirt, which he knew well, to tar, which he did not know at all, and finally, after that, the road changed to a total stranger just like his father. It was rocky, round-a-bout, up, down, and all around; a thing of potholes and rain pockets and so many twists and turns that Nesta could not count them.

While the bus raced down hill towards Brown's Town, Captain Marley never moved. His body, big and hot, was pressed against Nesta who, tiring of the scenery, soon fell asleep. When he woke, the bus had stopped. They had arrived in Kingston and the city lay harshly and brightly before them.

Nesta could not believe how large it was—wherever he looked the tenement jungle blotted the mountains, and the air was stifling. Yard smoke clotted the streets and Nesta's nose stung with the odor of burning rubber. The sun shone hard and clear, but it could not burn through the ashen haze, the dark daylight of Kingston.

Captain Marley led Nesta through a boiling sea of staring faces. Here was a world Nesta had never seen and could not imagine. As Captain Marley pulled him out of the way, two baggedy boys came by with their wooden handcarts of water coconuts, icies, and *bulla breads*. A fierce clamor rose up. All around them people pushed and bumped and shoved. Nesta felt small and unimportant beside the tall man who pulled him along through the crowd.

Wherever Nesta looked, he saw filth—trash. The gutter ran with an inky seepage. "Mind your shoes," Captain Marley ordered as he plowed down a narrow lane. Now the clatter of Spanish Town Bus Park fell behind them. They walked on. When Nesta slowed his pace, Captain Marley increased his. The military march continued until they came to an unpainted, rough-boarded cottage on a dark, dead-end street.

It started to rain. Captain Marley went up the stairs of the cottage, and, for the first time, he let go of Nesta's hand. Then he rapped on the door and a sad-eyed woman greeted them. Without asking, Nesta knew that this was the place where he and his father were going to live. However, he could not imagine the big-booted Captain staying in such a small, dingy house.

"I am Mrs. Gray," the old woman said. Nesta stood still as a post. Mrs. Gray, he thought, had a tired, kind face, but he did not want to go into her house, which even from the open door had a bad mildewy smell. Captain Marley exchanged a few words with Mrs. Gray. He put an envelope into her hand. Then, nodding briefly to Nesta, he turned and descended the stairs and walked down the rainy street.

Nesta stood alone with Mrs. Gray. His father faded into the rain and gloom. Mrs. Gray led Nesta inside. The cottage smelled of musty wood, old rotten cloth, and kerosene oil. "Is this where we're supposed to stay?" Nesta asked. Mrs. Gray answered, "Just you. Your father has his duties elsewhere."

Nesta did not want to go any farther into the strange, dark cottage. But Mrs. Gray led him along the narrow unlit hall to the kitchen out back. There, under a rain-beaten zinc roof, she took a black pot off the fire, and gave Nesta a bowl of pumpkin soup. As the rain banged down, he ate hungrily, wondering what Ciddy, Omeriah, and Alberta were doing, and whether it was raining back in Nine Miles.

That night Nesta slept on a *kaya* mattress in the same room as Mrs. Gray. The rain kept on and as he lay in the unfamiliar bedroom, he dreamed of raggamuffin beggars with hollow, graveyard eyes and old faded men with scraggly fishbone beards. But mostly, he had visions of his father in his brass-buttoned uniform, dark pressed pants, and tall shiny boots. Yet, in the dream, the Captain had no face. The dream changed. He saw himself riding Nimble, with his arms around the little donkey's neck, and the song of the crickets in his ear, and Omeriah walking close by.

Next morning, when Nesta woke up, Mrs. Gray was too sick to get out of bed. "Run a-market and carry come rice and *gungo pea*," she said feebly from her pillow. Nesta, all at once, was caring for the person who was supposed to be caring for him. But he followed her directions and ran to the nearby market she told him about. There he saw *higglers* with their goods spread out for all to see—huge, rough yams, strings of tangerines, hard green limes, june plums, *naseberries*, *soursop*, *sweetsop*, oranges, *ackee, calaloo*. All of these reminded Nesta of where he was from, the country.

He loved the market, not just because of the fruits and vegetables, but because of the music. The *higglers* did not only sell their things, they sang about them. "Hey, *bwai*," sang a little *beenie man*, "Touch me tomato, come touch me yam, pumpkin, potato." On the way back to Mrs. Gray's cottage, Nesta saw a *blackheart man*. He had seen them before, of course, up in the hills of St. Ann, but this one, with his long, ropy locks and fiery eyes, was living under the bridge in a hut made from a packing crate.

There were plenty of tales in Nine Miles about the *blackheart man* who stole your soul and carried it away in a crocus sack. Yet this dreadlock person was soft-spoken and nice, and when Nesta passed by his place, the *blackheart man* gave him a *doctor bird* woven from a piece of coconut leaf.

In the days and weeks that followed, Nesta grew quite independent. There was no question of his going to school—Mrs. Gray was too sick to be left alone. As the weeks turned into months, she got steadily worse. Finally, she was bedridden almost all of the time and Nesta was her only caregiver. However, he learned to do everything—cooking, cleaning, marketing. It was the last that he liked first and best, because, always, when he went to market, there was the *beenie man* who taught Nesta new songs.

One day the *beenie man* taught Nesta how to make a tiny one-stringed instrument out of a sardine tin. Another time, he taught him how to shape a cigar box into a guitar. The strings were made of palm twine and they made a sweet sound when you plucked them. But it was not all music on market day, much of what Nesta saw was hardship. Sometimes people fought over food. And some were really good at stealing it and running away.

So Nesta learned the truth of Omeriah's saying, "Rain does not fall on one man's house alone." He saw that everyone in Kingston was up against the same hard wall of poverty. No one was exempt from it. Being poor was the one thing that bound each to each, and all to all. Poverty, Nesta realized, stalked the streets of Kingston like a dragon. And right along beside it went the devil of hunger.

One night—after a long hard day at market—Nesta dreamed that he was living in the ancient city of Babylon. There, the rich lived on top of the poor and pressed them down like swollen grapes into the earth. Nesta woke that morning with a terrible, uneasy feeling and, again, he longed to be back in the sweet hills of St. Ann.

In the time that passed, Nesta was always by himself. Yet there was never a day, nor even an hour, when he did not think about Ciddy. And he never stopped wondering what Omeriah and Alberta were doing . . . whether the melons were ripening and the corn turning golden . . . whether Nimble was as sure-footed as ever—but where, oh, where was Mumma Ciddy?

Often when Nesta was daydreaming, he had visions of Ciddy. She was always standing there looking right at him, saying, "Nesta, my child, where are you?" He would snap out of it, hardly aware that it was a daydream—his sight was so clear and the picture of his mother so real. Occasionally, Nesta had thoughts of Captain Marley, whom he imagined as he last saw him striding roughly through the rain. But the Captain did not pay him a visit, not once.

One day when Nesta had been with Mrs. Gray for about a year, Ciddy walked into the yard, as if she had been doing so every day since the beginning of his stay in Kingston. Nesta could not believe his eyes. "Mumma, you fin'ly come!" He ran and hugged her and she hugged him and there were tears in her eyes. And in his, too.

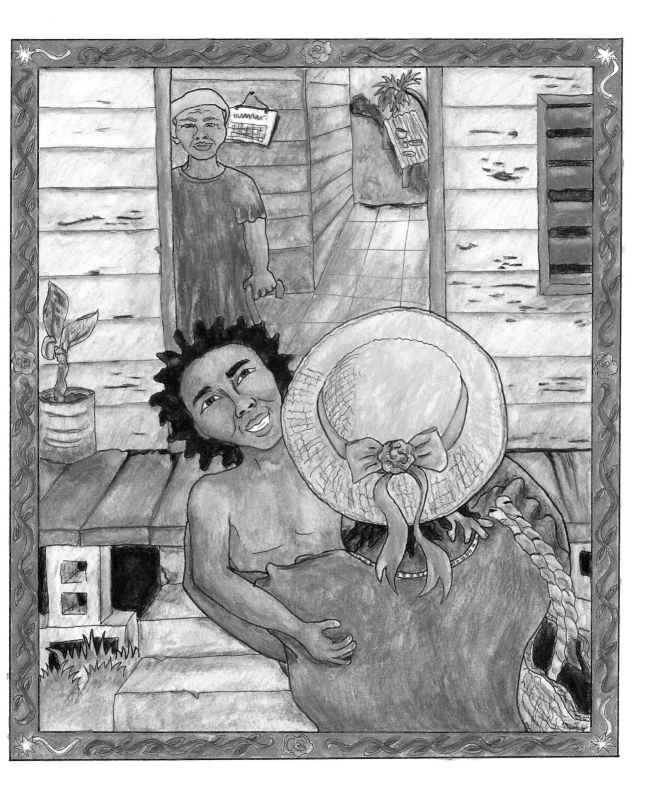

Mrs. Gray came trembling to the open door leaning on her cane. Ciddy shook her head and said angrily, "I have been looking for my Nesta up and down, ever since Captain took him away—kidnapped him."

Mrs. Gray protested, "He did no such thing. He intended Nesta to go to school." She lowered her eyes, and added, "I been too sick for that." Ciddy gave her an unforgiving stare. "It's not what you *intend* to do—it's what you *do*," she said, holding Nesta tight in her arms. Then she looked Mrs. Gray deeply in the eyes, and said, "So why you never write me about my son?"

For a moment Mrs. Gray was speechless. Then she asked, "How did you find my house?"

Ciddy replied, "A friend of ours, Maggy James, saw Nesta walking on Spanish Town Road, just yesterday. She told me and I came here at once, and I asked all around where Nesta lived, and no one seemed to know. Then a *blackheart man* living down by the bridge said, 'I know that boy.' It was him who brought me to your yard."

Mrs. Gray sighed, "I never thought Captain would keep my house so secret." She smiled weakly and said, "Nesta has been a lifesaver for me, and I don't think him any worse for wear."

"Let me look at you, child," Ciddy said, as she held Nesta at arm's length. He was taller, and older. And somehow, he seemed wiser. Something in his eyes. She wondered if this was what city life did to a country boy. Nesta looked like a little man, a boy still, but there was something so grown up about the way he stood, so straight and tall and sure of himself.

Mrs. Gray had spoken the truth when she said that Nesta was no worse for wear. "Can we go home now, Mumma?" Nesta asked. "Yes, baby," she said, "we are both going home now." And that is what they did. The two of them took the country bus back to Nine Miles, home to Omeriah and Alberta. Home to Nimble. Home.

"Prodigal son return!" Omeriah laughed when Nesta got off the bus, and stepped into the Nine Miles twilight. Here the *croaker lizards* were croaking, the rat bats were flying, and the frogs were singing. Nesta—one hand in Ciddy's and the other in Omeriah's—was glad to be alive and grateful to be home.

"Some people, Mumma," he said, as she tucked him into his own bed that night, "don't have a bed." Ciddy nodded and Alberta and Omeriah smiled. They looked knowingly at Nesta, who went on—"Even if you have a rockstone for a pillow, that could be your bed."

"Heavens," Alberta exclaimed, "you have grown so. Are you going to be a wise man now?"

"I am going to be a singer," Nesta smiled. Ciddy asked him if he knew any songs. So Nesta sang the song he had learned from the *beenie man* at the market. "Hey, mister, touch me tomato, touch me pumpkin and potato." Ciddy laughed. So did Omeriah and Alberta.

Omeriah asked, "How do you know you're going to be a singer?"

"Three little birdies tell me so," Nesta answered. But whether he was dreaming, teasing, or just talking, no one really knew, for by then he was already asleep. Yet the next morning he sang his favorite songs on Nimble's back, as he and Omeriah went to the farm. And from that day on, he never stopped singing.

Rise up this morning,
smile at the rising sun.
Three little birds
pitch by my doorstep
singing sweet songs
of melodies pure and true,
saying,
This is my message
to you-oo-oo . . .
singing,
don't worry about a thing,
cause every little thing
gonna be all right.
Don't worry about a thing,
cause every little thing
gonna be all right.

—Bob Marley

AFTERWORD

After spending most of his boyhood in Nine Miles, Bob Marley returned to Kingston with his mother. This time he lived in the Trench Town ghetto, where he took up his vow to be a singer and a writer of songs. Kingston during the seventies was a place of extreme poverty where the living conditions were among the worst in the third world. Bob Marley's optimistic vision taught people to be upfull—hopeful instead of hopeless.

Why should I bend down my head and cry?
Why should I bend down my head and cry?
The old world has ended.
The new world has just begun[1]

Bob found a mentor in Joe Higgs, who was a crucial Kingston musician and teacher. It was Joe who encouraged Bob to write, to sing, and to play the guitar. He also molded Bob, Peter McIntosh, and Bunny Livingston into a mellow-voiced trio called The Wailing Wailers. In the midst of Trench Town's race riots and food shortages, Bob Marley wrote diamond-hard, gritty poems to which he set a new rhythmic beat. The innovative style was called rock steady because it rolled like the sea. Whatever it was called—it was new.

Bob Marley's enduring vision set him apart from so many others who saw their world crumbling before them. After his first painful year in Kingston, Marley somehow knew that, as he wrote, "Every little thing is going be all right." This courageous view became his anthem. As times changed, rock steady turned into the simmering sound of reggae. Bob was the major force behind the music that reshuffled the rolling rhythm of rock steady and gave it a measured upbeat. Rita Anderson, soon to be Bob's wife, also joined the group. Two other female singers perfected the back-up vocalists who became the I-Threes—Rita Anderson, Judy Mowatt, and Marcia Griffiths.

Throughout the seventies, Bob Marley's name was identified with reggae music. His group grew into Bob Marley and the Wailers. Their reggae fusion was a forceful mixture of folk, jazz, and rhythm and blues. It was called roots music because it harkened back to Africa—the root of life for all Jamaicans. Another taproot of Marley's music was the Bible. Grandfather Omeriah's tales of Old Testament heroes and kings were a rich part of his childhood, and he used them them as a songwriter.

David slew Goliath with a sling and a stone;
Samson slew the Philistines with a donkey jawbone.[2]

By the late seventies, Bob Marley was the leading voice of his generation. But because of his revolutionary, Rastafarian views, he was a target for those who wanted to keep things as they were. The Rastafarian movement, which started in the 1930s when Haile Selassie I was crowned king in Ethiopia, was strong in Jamaica. Rastas believed that the emperor was a deity, as proven by his lineage from the biblical House of David. Further, Rastas carried the mystic faith that living simply and loving one another would make for redemption on Earth.

Bob Marley lived among elder Rastas, both in Kingston and in Nine Miles. He absorbed the Bible, meditated on its prescriptions of peace, and practiced what he preached. But he did not believe in bending down before the colonial rulers of the day. Jamaica still lived and operated under the shadow of colonial England. Bob's message was prophetically clear, "I do not come to bow; I come to conquer." While he did not mean this literally, he did intend it to be revolutionary.

To the conservative members of Jamaican society, Bob Marley was a real threat to the order of the day. It was no coincidence, then, that a band of hirelings tried to kill Marley on the night of December 5, 1976. They nearly succeeded. He was shot in the chest and arm, and his wife Rita was shot in the head. This did not stop him from appearing before thousands at the Smile Jamaica Concert in Kingston only two days later. While there, he unveiled his wounds so that everyone could see that he was all right.

Sometime after that concert, Bob sang at the One Love Peace Concert, also in Kingston, and, dancing amid forks of lightning and peals of thunder, he called for the two estranged political leaders, Edward Seaga and Michael Manley, to present themselves. While the storm crackled in the night sky, the two men came on stage. Bob Marley clasped their hands in his, binding them together and showing the audience that, in spite of their differences, diverse men can live as one. This was, in a sense, like a Rastafarian sacrament, proving that "one love, one heart" was not just a song lyric but a workable way of life. That, too, was the meaning behind Rasta. It was as a Rasta prophet that Marley rose in stature, some saying he was like Joseph in the Bible.

Throughout the late seventies and early eighties Bob Marley's influence as a Rasta and as a singer continued to grow. Although he died of cancer in 1981, his spirit lives in his music and in the work of his children. For celebrating the unification of all peoples throughout the world, Bob Marley was awarded Jamaica's Order of Merit and the United Nations Medal of Peace. He was also inducted into the Rock and Roll Hall of Fame. *Legend,* the most popular album of Bob Marley, has attained Diamond status with over 10 million copies sold since 1984. No single artist of the Caribbean has done more for African unity than Bob Marley, nor is any artist more commonly quoted on the street.

GLOSSARY

Ackee:

The national fruit of Jamaica. Traditionally cooked with salted codfish, this food is rarely eaten anywhere except on the island of Jamaica and other nations which have a large Jamaican population.

Beenie Man:

A reference to a person small in stature, like the little "beenie bird" that is also called a "quit" or "squit" in Jamaica.

Blackheart Man:

An old way of saying Rastafarian. Blackheart men of Jamaica allowed their locks to grow out, and their unusual appearance in the 1930s and 1940s struck fear into the hearts of some more conservative people. In fact, there were children's legends about blackheart men that might be compared to tales of trolls in Scandinavia; tales invoked whenever a misbehaving child was threatened, as in, "The *blackheart man's* gonna git you, if you don't mind your ways!"

Bulla Bread:

Round cake made with flour, molasses, baking soda, and ginger, known for its sweetness and toughness. Much enjoyed by school children and poor people and is often sold by *higglers* or at village shops all over the island.

Calaloo:

A West Indian leafy plant that resembles spinach and is part of every Jamaican's daily diet.

Croaker Lizard:

This member of the gecko family has large, round eyes with a pupil like a snake's. For many reasons, the folklore of the croaker is associated with ghosts. Croakers make a very loud, hoarse screech at night.

Doctor Bird:

This hummingbird is unique to Jamaica. It has a two-foot-long swallow tail. The bird's name comes from its resemblance to an eighteenth-century doctor's frock coat and from the Arawak belief that it was a medicinal creature.

Dreadlock:

Style of natural hair worn by members of the Rastafarian faith, but also an outgrowth of African tribal hair, as well. The appearance is long and straight and, some say, the equivalent of a lion's mane.

Gungo Pea:

A bean that grows on a shrub and is part of the Jamaican diet, usually mixed in soup or with rice.

Higgler:

A peddler in Jamaica and the backbone of the street sellers. Usually a hardy woman, but often a man, too.

John Crow:

Black plumed, red-skin head vulture who, legend tells, once reminded the Jamaican people of a certain unpopular, stiff-necked preacher. References to these birds are sometimes deathly, as that is what the bird eats—carrion.

Kaya Mattress:

Made from coconut husk or copra, this was the old-fashioned, or natural, mattress of country Jamaica.

Naseberry:

A small, brown, sweet, grainy fruit that is as well loved as it is common on the island.

Soursop:

A delicious fruit that is often prepared as a drink. It is known for its healthful benefits, one of which is calming the nerves.

Sweetsop:

Smaller than its country cousin, the soursop, the sweetsop is no less tasty, but is normally not made into a drink.

CHRONOLOGY

1945: Born Nesta Robert Marley, February 6, in Nine Miles, Parish of St. Ann, Jamaica.

1950: Lived one year in Kingston, Jamaica, with Mrs. Gray.

1951: Returned to the village of Nine Miles to live with his grandfather Omeriah, his grandmother Alberta, and his mother Cedella.

1955: Moved with Cedella to Trenchtown, Kingston. Bob became friends with Bunny Livingston, the son of Cedella's common-law husband, Toddy Livingston.

1959: Left school and became apprenticed to a welder. Began to make music with Bunny Livingston on a sardine-can guitar.

1961-1962: Recorded "Judge Not," a song inspired by his grandfather, at Leslie Kong's studio in Kingston.

1962-1963: Founded The Wailin' Wailers with Bunny Livingston and Peter Tosh. "Simmer Down" released.

1966: Married Rita Anderson, realized he was a Rastafarian ("since creation").

1971: Signed recording contract with Chris Blackwell of Island Records.

1973: Released first album *Catch A Fire,* followed by *Burnin'* later that year. In the next decade, he completed 10 award-winning albums.

1976: Wounded in an assassination attempt at his 56 Hope Road home, two days later performed in Smile Jamaica Concert.

1977: Injured playing football and diagnosed with melanoma.

1978: Received the United Nations Medal of Peace.

1981: Awarded Order of Merit, Jamaica's high honor. Left the world on 11 May in Miami, Florida. Given an official state funeral in the village of Nine Miles where he was born.

DISCOGRAPHY

Major albums by Bob Marley produced by Chris Blackwell; Bob Marley and the Wailers; Stephen Marley and Tuff Gong International:

1972 *Catch A Fire*

1973 *Burnin'*

1974 *Natty Dread*

1975 *Live! Bob Marley and the Wailers*

1976 *Rastaman Vibration*

1977 *Exodus*

1978 *Kaya*

1978 *Babylon by Bus*

1979 *Survival*

1980 *Uprising*

1983 *Confrontation*

1984 *Legend*

1986 *Rebel Music*

1991 *Talkin' Blues*

1995 *Natural Mystic*

1992 *Songs of Freedom*

1997 *Dreams of Freedom*

1999 *Chant Down Babylon*

2001 *One Love—The Very Best of Bob Marley and the Wailers*

ENDNOTES: SONG ATTRIBUTION

Songs by Bob Marley.

[1]Why Should I

[2]Rastaman Live Up

Hampton Roads Publishing Company is dedicated to providing quality
children's books that stimulate the intellect,
teach valuable lessons, and allow our children's spirits to grow.
We have created our line of *Young Spirit Books* for the evolving
human spirit of our children. Give your children
Young Spirit Books—their key to a whole new world!

Hampton Roads Publishing Company

. . . for the evolving human spirit

Hampton Roads Publishing Company
publishes books on a variety of subjects,
including metaphysics, health, integrative medicine,
visionary fiction, and other related topics.

For a copy of our latest catalog, call toll-free
(800) 766-8009, or send your name and address to:

Hampton Roads Publishing Company, Inc.
1125 Stoney Ridge Road
Charlottesville, VA 22902

e-mail: hrpc@hrpub.com
Website: www.hrpub.com